TOP 10 POWER PITCHERS

BY K. C. KELLEY

Published by The Child's World®
1980 Lookout Drive • Mankato, MN 56003-1705
800-599-READ • www.childsworld.com

Photo credits:
Alamy Stock Photo: Everett Collection 13; AP Photo:
David Durochik 6, 18; 14; David J. Phillip 17; Bill
Janscha 19. Dreamstime.com: Stephen McSweeny
21. Library of Congress: 12. Newscom: Mark LoMi-
glio/Icon SMI CCX 7; Glenn Osmundson/KRT 8; TSN/
Icon SMI 9; John Cordes/Icon Sportswire 10, 15; Cliff
Welch/Icon SMI 11; Art Foxall/UPI 16; Shutterstock:
Kevin Grant (cover), 1.

ISBN: 9781503827264
LCCN: 2017960463

Printed in the United States of America
PA02380

CONTENTS

Introduction: Who's Number One?. 4

Steve Carlton. 6

Aroldis Chapman 7

Roger Clemens 8

Bob Gibson. 9

Pedro Martinez 10

Tom Seaver 11

Walter Johnson. 12

Sandy Koufax 14

Randy Johnson 16

Nolan Ryan. 18

Your Top Ten! 20

Sports Glossary 22

Find Out More .23

Index/About the Author 24

WHO'S NUMBER ONE?

At the end of most baseball games, everyone knows who won. It's the team with the most runs!

At the end of the World Series, the No. 1 team is clear, too. It's the winner of the final game . . . and there's always a winner. So finding the top baseball team is easy. Choosing the greatest power pitcher of all time is a bit harder. Is it the guy with the most strikeouts? Or the pitcher who threw the hardest? Or is it the hurler who batters feared most? Fans, experts, and fellow players all have their opinions.

Opinions are different than facts. Facts are real things. Nolan Ryan had 5,714 strikeouts. That's a fact. Baseball is the greatest sport in the world. That's an opinion. The distance from the mound to home plate is 60 feet, 6 inches in the majors. That's a fact. Chicago's Wrigley Field is the best place to watch a baseball game. That's an opinion.

Tom Seaver

NUMBERS, NUMBERS

Most Career Strikeouts
(through 2017)

1. Nolan Ryan	5,714
2. Randy Johnson	4,875
3. Roger Clemens	4.672
4. Steve Carlton	4,136
5. Bert Blyleven	3,701

Some people might think baseball is not that great. (I know: Can you believe it?) But that's fine; that's their opinion. However, they can't say Nolan Ryan didn't rack up those strikeouts. That's a fact. Cubs fans think Wrigley is No. 1. But you would find a very different opinion in lots of other ballparks, where fans think THEIR place is No. 1.

And that's where you come in. You get to choose who is the greatest power pitcher ever. You will read lots of facts and stories about these great players. Based on that, what's your opinion? Who's No. 1? There are no wrong answers . . . but you might have some fun discussions with your baseball-loving pals! Then again, you might just pick the guy with the MOST strikeouts . . . it's up to you!

Read on and then after you're done, make up your own Top 10 list.

Sandy Koufax

STEVE CARLTON

CARDINALS • PHILLIES

Teammates called him "Lefty." Opponents called him "scary!" Steve Carlton started his career on the Cardinals and helped them win World Series in 1967. He moved to the Phillies and became a great pitcher on a really bad team. In 1972, he won 27 games to lead the NL. The Phillies only won 59! How bad would they have been without him? That year he also had a career-high 310 strikeouts and led the NL with a 1.97 ERA.

Lefty helped his team improve and they made the playoffs six times. He led the Phils to a World Series title in 1980. Against the Royals, he won two games, including the Series-clinching sixth game.

Lefty was a strikeout machine. He also had a fantastic slider. He won four **Cy Young awards** and led the NL in strikeouts five times.

Pittsburgh slugger Willie Stargell on hitting against Carlton: "It's like drinking coffee with a fork."

NUMBERS, NUMBERS

Unlike today's pitchers, Lefty pitched a lot! He led the NL in innings five times. He topped 250 innings in 12 seasons!

AROLDIS CHAPMAN

REDS * YANKEES * CUBS

Many fans judge pitchers by how fast they throw. A machine called a **radar gun** measures how fast. And no one is faster than Aroldis Chapman. His long left arm and tall frame help him power the ball to the plate like no one else. In 2013, Chapman threw a pitch that went 105.1 miles per hour!

Chapman was born in Cuba. That nation does not let its citizens play in the Majors. Players have to sneak out to play. Chapman did just that and joined the Cincinnati Reds in 2010. Soon he was a top **closer**.

In 2016, he joined the Cubs and helped them win their first World Series since 1908. His power pitching was key to their success. Chapman moved to the Yankees in 2017.

NUMBERS, NUMBERS

2017: Strikeouts Per 9 Innings
(at least 50 innings pitched)

1. Craig Kimbrel, Red Sox		15.8
2. Dellin Betances, Yankees		15.1
3. Corey Knebel, Brewers		14.9
4. Kenley Janse, Dodgers		14.4
5. Kirby Yates, Padres		14.0

Chapman has six seasons with more than 35 **saves**. More and more, teams need a player who can close the door in the ninth and earn a save.

ROGER CLEMENS

RED SOX • BLUE JAYS • YANKEES • ASTROS

Few pitchers were ever as feared as Roger "Rocket" Clemens. In 1986, only his third season, he was the AL MVP and Cy Young Award winner. He earned two more Cy Youngs for the Red Sox. Clemens moved to the Toronto Blue Jays in 1997 and was even better. He won pitching's **Triple Crown** and another Cy Young Award. With the Yankees, he won a pair of World Series in 1999 and 2000. In 2004, he returned to his native Texas. With Houston, he won his seventh Cy Young Award with an 18–4 record.

However, Clemens is not in the Hall of Fame. Most experts believe that later in his career he used illegal drugs. These might have helped him pitch better. Did the Rocket need them? Probably not. But if he used them, he disappointed many fans.

In a 1986 game, Clemens tied a Major League record by striking out 20 batters. Then he became the first to do that twice! He fanned 20 in a 1996 game.

NUMBERS, NUMBERS

Rocket's League-Leading Stats
ERA: 7 times
Wins: 4 times
Strikeouts: 5 times

BOB GIBSON

CARDINALS

When Bob Gibson took the mound, everyone had to get out of the way. Batters feared his fastball. He was also not afraid to pitch inside, near the batters. Catchers had to watch out, too. When Cardinals catchers tried to talk to him during a game, all they got was a glare! "Gibby" was tough, powerful, and determined.

Gibson pitched for the Cardinals for 17 years and was an eight-time All-Star. His best season came in 1968. He had a 1.12 ERA and led the NL with 268 strikeouts. He was named the Cy Young Award winner and the NL MVP. Gibson also won nine **Gold Gloves** as the best-fielding pitcher.

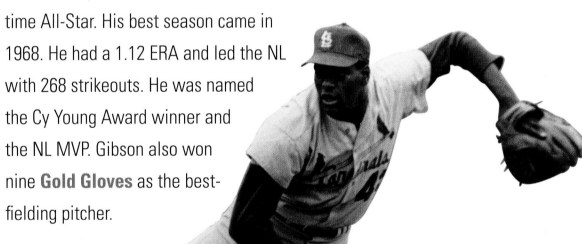

How good an athlete was Gibson? Before he played with the Cardinals, he shot hoops for the famous Harlem Globetrotters.

NUMBERS, NUMBERS

Lowest Single-Season ERA since 1900

1. Dutch Leonard, 0.96 (1914)
2. Mordecai Brown, 1.04 (1906)
3. Bob Gibson, 1.12 (1968)
4. Christy Mathewson, 1.14 (1909)
5. Walter Johnson, 1.14 (1913)

PEDRO MARTINEZ

EXPOS • RED SOX • METS

Pedro Martinez had a secret weapon. His fingers were longer than usual. That let him put just a bit more power and spin on his pitches. Also, few pitchers ever wanted to win more than Pedro.

He won his first Cy Young Award with Montreal in 1997 with a 1.90 ERA. In 1999, playing for Boston, he won the pitching Triple Crown and two more Cy Young Awards. In 2004, he helped the Red Sox win their first World Series since 1918! How dominant was he? From 1997 to the end of his career in 2009, Martinez never lost more than nine games in a season. His fastball piled up the strikeouts, but his curveball and slider were legendary!

Martinez had six seasons with a WHIP of less than one. What's WHIP? It stands for wins + hits per inning pitched. His career WHIP is 1.05, sixth-best since 1900!

NUMBERS, NUMBERS

Martinez won 219 games and lost only 100. That's a .687 winning percentage—fourth-best for any pitcher since 1900!

TOM SEAVER

METS • REDS • RED SOX

In a 1969 game, Seaver came within two outs of a perfect game He also had a no-hitter in 1978.

Tom Seaver put everything he had into every pitch. He was famous for throwing so hard, his right knee scraped the dirt.

He was a star pitcher in college at USC. He joined the New York Mets in 1967 and was Rookie of the Year. In 1969, he won 25 games! He helped the Mets win their first World Series. Seaver also won his first of three Cy Young Awards.

Seaver's best pitch was a powerful fastball. He led the NL in strikeouts five times. He also led in ERA three times.

Seaver left the Mets in 1977 and played for the Reds, White Sox, and Red Sox. With Boston in 1986, he won his 300th career game.

NUMBERS, NUMBERS
Seaver was durable. He had nine seasons with 14 or more complete games. These days, a pitcher might lead his league with only three or four such games.

WALTER JOHNSON

WASHINGTON SENATORS

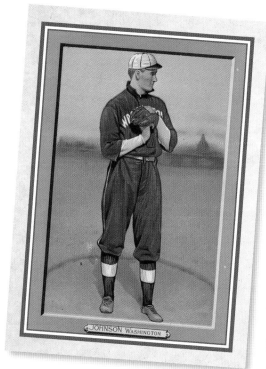

Walter Johnson's nickname was "The Big Train." At the time, trains were the fastest thing around. So was Johnson's fastball. They didn't have radar guns back then, so we don't know exactly how fast he threw. The best players in the game couldn't hit him, though.

Johnson didn't look like he was throwing hard. He had an easy, slow motion with his arm. Sometimes, he threw sidearm. As he finished his delivery, the ball seemed to leap from his hand. It blew past hitter after hitter! Johnson retired in 1927. His 3,509 strikeouts were the most ever to that point. He held the record until 1983! That's a pretty big train!

He was not just about strikeouts. He kept hitters off the bases by allowing very few hits and walks. Johnson won 20 or more games in 12 seasons, including seven years with 25 or more Ws! How important was he to his team, the Washington Senators? A new stat called Wins Above Replacement (WAR) has the answer.

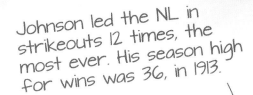

Johnson led the NL in strikeouts 12 times, the most ever. His season high for wins was 36, in 1913.

WAR measures how hard it would be to replace any player. In that category, Johnson led the AL nine times. That means he was more important to his team than any other hitter or pitcher in the league.

Johnson's most famous year was 1924. He led the Washington Senators to the World Series title. In Game 6, he came on in **relief** to close out the clinching game.

The Big Train won 417 games in his career, the second most all-time. He was one of the first five players elected to the Baseball Hall of Fame in 1936.

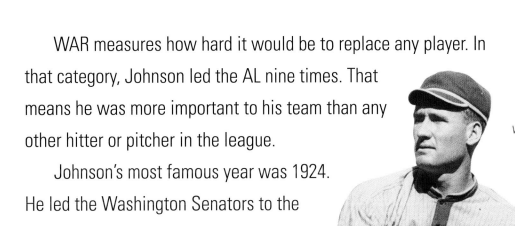

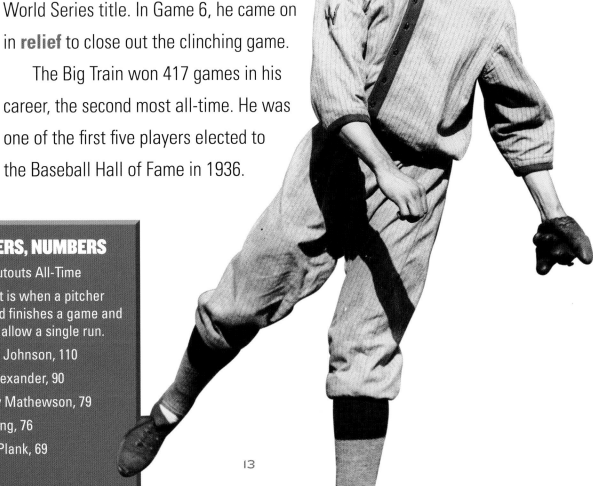

NUMBERS, NUMBERS

Most Shutouts All-Time

A shutout is when a pitcher starts and finishes a game and does not allow a single run.

1. Walter Johnson, 110
2. G.C. Alexander, 90
3. Christy Mathewson, 79
4. Cy Young, 76
5. Eddie Plank, 69

SANDY KOUFAX

DODGERS

Was Sandy Koufax the best pitcher ever? Many experts think so. More people might agree if he had pitched longer. Koufax was forced to retire at the age of 30 with an injured elbow. When he was healthy, though, wow . . . what a pitcher!

Koufax began playing with the Brooklyn Dodgers in 1955. The team moved to Los Angeles in 1959. Koufax threw the ball very hard, but he was **wild**. He was still learning to control his great speed.

Starting in 1961, Koufax figured it out. His fastball became more lively and he learned an awesome curveball.

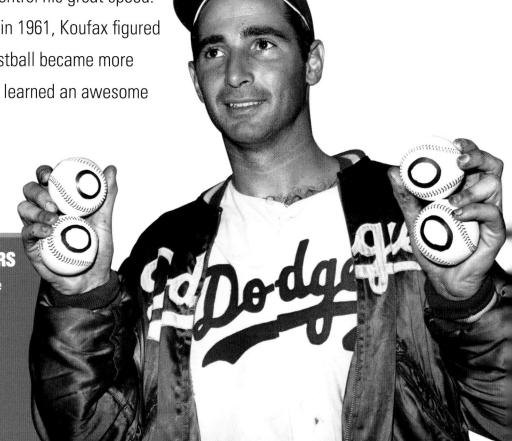

NUMBERS, NUMBERS
Most No-Hitters, All-Time
1. Nolan Ryan, 7
2. Sandy Koufax, 4
3. Bob Feler, 3
4. Larry Corcoran, 3
5. Cy Young, 3

In 1965, Koufax chose not to pitch in a key World Series game. The reason? The game was played on a Jewish holiday. Koufax chose his faith over baseball and became a hero to many.

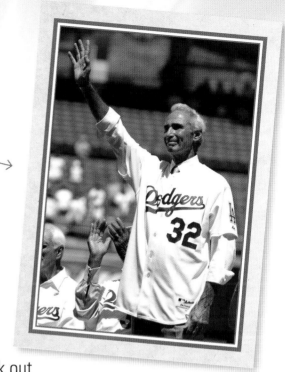

For the next six seasons, there might not have been a better pitcher.

He won three pitching Triple Crowns (1963, 1965, and 1966). Three times he won more than 25 games. He led the NL in strikeouts four times. In 1965, he struck out 382 batters. That set a single-season record not broken until 1983.

Koufax led the Dodgers to a World Series championship in 1963. He won two games against the Yankees in that series.

In 1965, Koufax pitched his best game ever. Against the Cubs at Dodger Stadium, he did not let a single player reach base. The Dodgers did just enough to help him, getting only one hit. It was a perfect game!

L.A. capped off that season by beating the Twins in the World Series as Koufax won a pair of games.

Koufax won his third Cy Young Award in 1966. That season, after the Dodgers lost the World Series to Baltimore, Koufax had to leave the game he loved. He was an easy choice for the Baseball Hall of Fame. Since then, he has helped coach and mentor many young Dodgers players.

RANDY JOHNSON

MARINERS • DIAMONDBACKS • ASTROS

At 6-10, Randy Johnson was the tallest player ever when he took the mound in 1988. By the end of his great career, he stood tall in many other areas. "The Big Unit" was one of the most overpowering pitchers in the game.

He started with the Montreal Expos in 1988 and moved to Seattle in 1989. He threw in the high 90s or even above 100 mph. But he was wild. He led the AL in walks three times. If you can't throw it over the plate, it doesn't matter how fast you throw!

Johnson worked hard and learned better control. In 1993, he won 19 games and led the AL with 308 strikeouts. In 1995, he led the AL in ERA and won his first Cy Young Award.

Johnson threw a perfect game in 2004. He did not allow a baserunner for the Braves. At the age of 40, he was the oldest perfect-game pitcher ever!

NUMBERS, NUMBERS

In 16 seasons, Johnson averaged more than 10 strikeouts for every nine innings he pitched!

The mighty hurler was traded to Houston during the 1998 season. He won 10 games for the Astros and helped them make the playoffs. He signed with Arizona in 1999 and began his best stretch. Over the next four seasons, he was the best pitcher in baseball. Johnson won four straight Cy Young Awards (1999–2003), while also leading in strikeouts all four seasons. (In total, he led his league in Ks nine times!)

His biggest season came in 2001. Teamed with fellow ace Curt Schilling, Johnson led Arizona to the World Series. There he won three games! He started and won two. Then in Game 7, he came on in relief to shut down the Yankees! The Big Unit was named the World Series MVP.

Johnson later played for the Yankees for two seasons and helped them reach the playoffs twice. He pitched until he was 45, firing fastballs past players as young as 20! In his final season, 2009, he won his 300th career game.

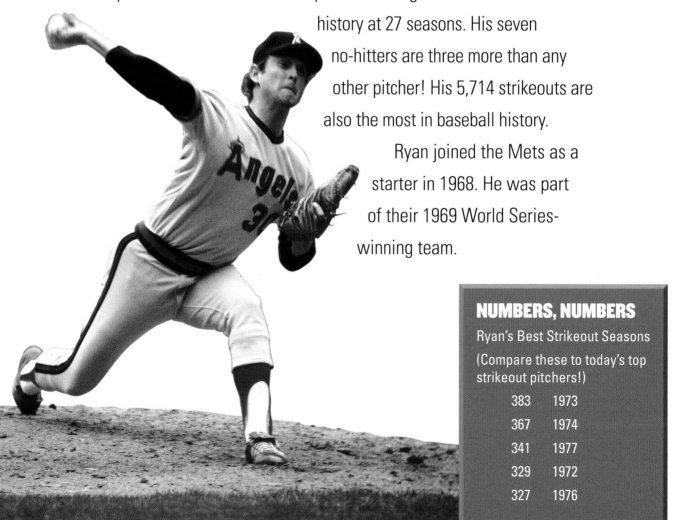

NOLAN RYAN

METS • ANGELS • ASTROS • RANGERS

Throughout his long, amazing career, Nolan Ryan struck out a LOT of hitters. Unfortunately, he also walked a LOT of hitters. Ryan had a stunning fastball, but hitters could often avoid it. He led the league in strikeouts nine times. He also led the league in walks eight times! But Ryan stuck with it and ended up with the longest career in baseball history at 27 seasons. His seven no-hitters are three more than any other pitcher! His 5,714 strikeouts are also the most in baseball history.

Ryan joined the Mets as a starter in 1968. He was part of their 1969 World Series–winning team.

NUMBERS, NUMBERS

Ryan's Best Strikeout Seasons
(Compare these to today's top strikeout pitchers!)

383	1973
367	1974
341	1977
329	1972
327	1976

One of Ryan's nicknames was "The Express." For a while, he owned part of a minor league team named for him: The Red Rock Express.

Nolan Ryan moved to the Angels in 1972 and had some of his best seasons. In 1973, he set a modern-day record with 383 strikeouts. That beat Koufax's 382 for the best since 1900. With the Angels, he had four seasons with 19 or more wins, including a career-high 22 in 1974.

In 1973, Ryan threw a no-hitter against the Royals. He would throw his last no-no in 1991 at the age of 44. In that game, he struck out 16 Blue Jays. Not bad for an "old" man!

In 1980, Ryan returned to his native Texas to pitch for the Astros. He led the NL in ERA twice, plus strikeouts three times. In 1989, he switched to the Texas Rangers and led the AL with 301 strikeouts at the age of 42. That gave him five 300-K seasons, the most ever!

Nolan Ryan just kept firing fastballs until he retired in 1993. His 27 MLB seasons are the most ever (as are his 2,795 walks!).

Ryan stayed in baseball and helped run the Rangers and Astros. In 2017, he watched proudly as Houston won its first World Series.

YOUR TOP TEN!

In this book, we listed our Top 10 in no particular order. We gave you some facts and information about each player. Now it's your turn to put the pitchers in order. Find a pen and paper. Now make your own list! Who should be the No. 1 power pitcher of all time? How about your other nine choices? Would they be the same players as we chose? Would they be in the same order? Are any players missing from this book? Who would you include? Put them in order—it's your call!

Remember, there are no wrong answers. Every fan might have different choices in a different order. Every fan should be able to back up their choices, though. If you need more information, go online and learn. Or find other books about these great players. Then discuss the choices with your friends!

THINK ABOUT THIS...

Here are some things to think about when making your own Top 10 list:

- How hard did he pitch?
- How many strikeouts did he have?
- Did the player help his team win?
- What made him such a great power pitcher?

20

SPORTS GLOSSARY

closer (KLOH-zer) a relief pitcher who finishes a winning game

Cy Young Award (SY YUNG uh-WARD) given to the top pitcher in each league; named for the all-time leader in wins with 511

fanned (FAND) slang for striking a batter out; comes from the wind a bat makes as it misses the ball!

Gold Gloves (GOLD GLUVS) awards given to the top fielder at each position on the field in each league

no-hitter (no-HITT-er) a game in which the starting pitcher does not allow a hit and wins the game

perfect game (PERF-ekt GAYM) a game in which the starting pitcher does not allow a single baserunner and wins the game

radar gun (RAY-dahr GUN) a device that measures how fast something moves in miles per hour

relief (ruh-LEEF) when a pitcher replaces another pitcher during a game

saves (SAYVZ) stats that record when a relief pitcher finishes a winning game

Triple Crown (TRIPP-ul KROWN) award for a pitcher who leads his league in wins, ERA, and strikeouts

wild (WYLD) in baseball, when a pitcher has trouble throwing strikes

FIND OUT MORE

IN THE LIBRARY

Aretha, David. *Top 10 Pitchers in Baseball*. New York, NY: Enslow Publishing, 2016.

Christopher, Matt. *On the Mound With . . . Randy Johnson*. New York, NY: Little, Brown, 2009.

Winter, Jonah. *You Never Heard of Sandy Koufax?* New York, NY: Random House, 2009.

ON THE WEB

Visit our Web site for links about Top 10 power pitchers: **childsworld.com/links**

Note to Parents, Teachers, and Librarians: We routinely verify our Web links to make sure they are safe and active sites. So encourage your readers to check them out!

INDEX

Arizona Diamondbacks, 17
Boston Red Sox, 8, 10, 11
Brooklyn Dodgers, 12
California Angels, 19
Carlton, Steve, 6
Chapman, Aroldis, 7
Chicago Cubs, 7
Cincinnati Reds, 7
Clemens, Roger "Rocket," 8
Cuba, 7
Gibson, Bob, 9
Houston Astros, 19
Johnson, Randy, 16-17
Johnson, Walter, 12-13
Koufax, Sandy, 14-15
Los Angeles Dodgers, 13

Martinez, Pedro 10
Montreal Expos, 10, 16
New York Mets, 11
New York Yankees, 7, 8, 17
Philadelphia Phillies, 6
Ryan, Nolan, 4, 18-19
St. Louis Cardinals, 6, 9
Schilling, Curt, 17
Seattle Mariners, 16
Seaver, Tom, 11
Texas Rangers, 19
Toronto Blue Jays, 8
Washington Senators, 12
World Series, 4, 6, 7, 10, 11, 13, 15, 17, 19
Wrigley Field, 4

ABOUT THE AUTHOR

K. C. Kelley has been an editor and writer for *Sports Illustrated* and the National Football League. He has written more than 150 books for young readers. He has coached Little League and Pony League baseball, but none of his pitchers could throw as fast as the players in this book. His favorite team is the Boston Red Sox.